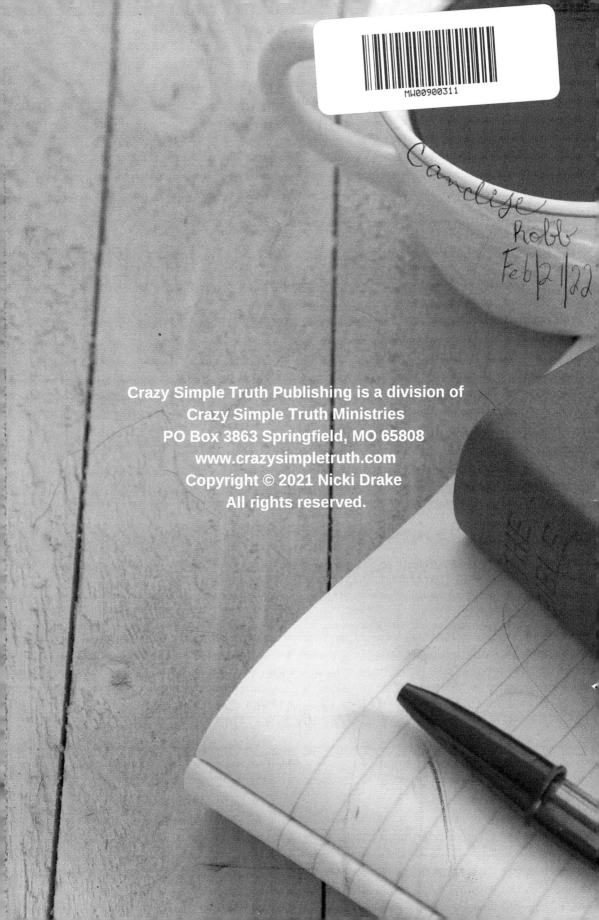

Date:

Who is the author or who is speaking in this verse?

John is the author

Fellowship of God

Verse:
If we say, "We have no sin" we are deciving ourselves, and the truth is not in us. If we confess our sins, He is faithful and righteous to forgive us our sins and to cleanse us from all unrighteousness

Did I learn anything that I can praise God for?
6. He is Faithful &
Righteous

He Forgives us of our sins

He cleanses us

from unrighteous

Did God tug at my heart about something I need to confess?
" If we say" We have no sin" we are decievuhy ourselves.

We need to confess our sins

What did I realize that I need to thank God for?

I need to thank him for being faithful and righteous. And that he cleanses my heart.

I am thankful because he's always going to continue to be our healing hands & be there.

What did I <u>realize</u> that I need God's help with?

⌐ At confessing my "BIG" sins
└ 5 things. I need to let go of.
Learn to be honest with GOD & pray
lay with the truth Day\Night.

Write a prayer and let God know how you plan to apply these lessons and truths to your life:

I promise to have more faith in Jesus to be more open with my guilt.
To put it all out there is my Biggest fears.
I would like to have more of a connection with Him.
I tend to hold on to hardships I do wanna let go of.

In the Almighty Name of Jesus I pray, Amen

Date: MAR/14/2022

Who is the author or who is speaking in this verse?

a psalms of David

Verse:
Have mercy upon me, O God,
According to your loving kindness;
According to the multitude of
Your tender mercies, Blot out
my transgressions.
Wash me throughly from my
iniquity, and cleanse
me from my Sin

Did I learn anything that I can praise God for?

I can praise him for having a
loving kindness
- Has mercy
- He cleanses me of sin

Did God tug at my heart about something I need to confess?

He tugged at my heart because;
○ live a life of sin
⤷ That I wanna change my ways
○ I'd like for him to give me
mercy whul sin

What did I realize that I need to thank God for?

o I'd like to give him thanks for accepting me as I and giving me time to show I too want to be more like him.

o Without him I'd be lost
↳ thank you for leading me in a better direction

What did I realize that I need God's help with?

o To have a openminded way of thinking
o To stop thinking & over working
o I need help with doing 1 thing at a time
o Try loving myself more.

Write a prayer and let God know how you plan to apply these lessons and truths to your life:

father thank you so much for being such a loving Father and I know you are always there to show me the way to be. Father please have mercy on me as I am learning to better me & my family & try at growing more like you daily.

Date: July 17, 2022

Who is the author or who is speaking in this verse?

house of David

Verse:

Sing to the Lord, you saints of his; praise his holy name. For his anger lasts only a moment, but his favor lasts a lifetime; Weeping may remain for a night, but rejoicing comes in the morning.

Did I learn anything that I can praise God for?

To sing to the Lord & Praise His Holy named for ~~it~~ He has good will for us.

God's anger does not last
His Favor is His hands, that are open.

Did God tug at my heart about something I need to confess?

That I'm not being more disiplined.
And I'm not praising His enough

What did I realize that I need to thank God for?

even tho I always don't see what is going on but God sees
He might only be angry for a minute I thank Him for that because there could be other things He could of done.
I praise Him for having love & time for us.
maybe I should see pass the wrong in my life & to know I have a place with Him.

What did I realize that I need God's help with?

- More praise
- have more time w Him
- The Hardships I'm facing

Write a prayer and let God know how you plan to apply these lessons and truths to your life:

Father God, I pray that I'm thankful for you in all that you do because without you I won't see I pray that you believe in each and everyone of us I pray that I'll PRAISE YOU MORE I want to learn t accept & thankful t whatever it may lost or changes in Be favors from you o Lord.

In Jesus name

In the Almighty Name of Jesus I pray, Amen

Date:

In the Almighty Name of Jesus I pray, Amen

Date:

Who is the author or who is speaking in this verse?

Verse:

Did I learn anything that I can praise God for?

Did God tug at my heart about something I need to confess?

What did I realize that I need to thank God for?

What did I realize that I need God's help with?

Write a prayer and let God know how you plan to apply these lessons
and truths to your life:

In the Almighty Name of Jesus I pray, Amen

Date:

Who is the author or who is speaking in this verse?

Verse:

Did I learn anything that I can praise God for?

Did God tug at my heart about something I need to confess?

What did I realize that I need to thank God for?

What did I realize that I need God's help with?

Write a prayer and let God know how you plan to apply these lessons and truths to your life:

In the Almighty Name of Jesus I pray, Amen

Date:

Who is the author or who is speaking in this verse?

Verse:

Did I learn anything that I can praise God for?

Did God tug at my heart about something I need to confess?

What did I realize that I need to thank God for?

What did I realize that I need God's help with?

Write a prayer and let God know how you plan to apply these lessons
and truths to your life:

In the Almighty Name of Jesus I pray, Amen

Date:

Who is the author or who is speaking in this verse?

Verse:

Did I learn anything that I can praise God for?

Did God tug at my heart about something I need to confess?

What did I realize that I need to thank God for?

What did I realize that I need God's help with?

Write a prayer and let God know how you plan to apply these lessons
and truths to your life:

In the Almighty Name of Jesus I pray, Amen

Date:

Who is the author or who is speaking in this verse?

Verse:

Did I learn anything that I can praise God for?

Did God tug at my heart about something I need to confess?

What did I realize that I need to thank God for?

What did I realize that I need God's help with?

Write a prayer and let God know how you plan to apply these lessons
and truths to your life:

In the Almighty Name of Jesus I pray, Amen

Date:

Who is the author or who is speaking in this verse?

Verse:

Did I learn anything that I can praise God for?

Did God tug at my heart about something I need to confess?

What did I realize that I need to thank God for?

What did I realize that I need God's help with?

Write a prayer and let God know how you plan to apply these lessons and truths to your life:

In the Almighty Name of Jesus I pray, Amen

Date:

Who is the author or who is speaking in this verse?

Verse:

Did I learn anything that I can praise God for?

Did God tug at my heart about something I need to confess?

What did I realize that I need to thank God for?

What did I realize that I need God's help with?

Write a prayer and let God know how you plan to apply these lessons
and truths to your life:

In the Almighty Name of Jesus I pray, Amen

Date:

Who is the author or who is speaking in this verse?

Verse:

Did I learn anything that I can praise God for?

Did God tug at my heart about something I need to confess?

What did I realize that I need to thank God for?

What did I realize that I need God's help with?

Write a prayer and let God know how you plan to apply these lessons
and truths to your life:

In the Almighty Name of Jesus I pray, Amen

Date:

Who is the author or who is speaking in this verse?

Verse:

Did I learn anything that I can praise God for?

Did God tug at my heart about something I need to confess?

What did I realize that I need to thank God for?

What did I realize that I need God's help with?

Write a prayer and let God know how you plan to apply these lessons and truths to your life:

In the Almighty Name of Jesus I pray, Amen

Date:

Who is the author or who is speaking in this verse?

Verse:

Did I learn anything that I can praise God for?

Did God tug at my heart about something I need to confess?

What did I realize that I need to thank God for?

What did I realize that I need God's help with?

Write a prayer and let God know how you plan to apply these lessons
and truths to your life:

In the Almighty Name of Jesus I pray, Amen

Date:

Who is the author or who is speaking in this verse?

Verse:

Did I learn anything that I can praise God for?

Did God tug at my heart about something I need to confess?

What did I realize that I need to thank God for?

What did I realize that I need God's help with?

Write a prayer and let God know how you plan to apply these lessons
and truths to your life:

In the Almighty Name of Jesus I pray, Amen

Date:

Who is the author or who is speaking in this verse?

Verse:

Did I learn anything that I can praise God for?

Did God tug at my heart about something I need to confess?

What did I realize that I need to thank God for?

What did I realize that I need God's help with?

Write a prayer and let God know how you plan to apply these lessons
and truths to your life:

In the Almighty Name of Jesus I pray, Amen

Date:

Who is the author or who is speaking in this verse?

Verse:

Did I learn anything that I can praise God for?

Did God tug at my heart about something I need to confess?

What did I realize that I need to thank God for?

What did I realize that I need God's help with?

Write a prayer and let God know how you plan to apply these lessons
and truths to your life:

In the Almighty Name of Jesus I pray, Amen

Date:

Who is the author or who is speaking in this verse?

Verse:

Did I learn anything that I can praise God for?

Did God tug at my heart about something I need to confess?

What did I realize that I need to thank God for?

What did I realize that I need God's help with?

Write a prayer and let God know how you plan to apply these lessons and truths to your life:

In the Almighty Name of Jesus I pray, Amen

Date:

Who is the author or who is speaking in this verse?

Verse:

Did I learn anything that I can praise God for?

Did God tug at my heart about something I need to confess?

What did I realize that I need to thank God for?

What did I realize that I need God's help with?

Write a prayer and let God know how you plan to apply these lessons and truths to your life:

In the Almighty Name of Jesus I pray, Amen

Date:

Who is the author or who is speaking in this verse?

Verse:

Did I learn anything that I can praise God for?

Did God tug at my heart about something I need to confess?

What did I realize that I need to thank God for?

What did I realize that I need God's help with?

Write a prayer and let God know how you plan to apply these lessons
and truths to your life:

In the Almighty Name of Jesus I pray, Amen

Date:

Who is the author or who is speaking in this verse?

Verse:

Did I learn anything that I can praise God for?

Did God tug at my heart about something I need to confess?

What did I realize that I need to thank God for?

What did I realize that I need God's help with?

Write a prayer and let God know how you plan to apply these lessons
and truths to your life:

In the Almighty Name of Jesus I pray, Amen

Date:

Who is the author or who is speaking in this verse?

Verse:

Did I learn anything that I can praise God for?

Did God tug at my heart about something I need to confess?

What did I realize that I need to thank God for?

What did I realize that I need God's help with?

Write a prayer and let God know how you plan to apply these lessons
and truths to your life:

In the Almighty Name of Jesus I pray, Amen

Date:

Who is the author or who is speaking in this verse?

Verse:

Did I learn anything that I can praise God for?

Did God tug at my heart about something I need to confess?

What did I realize that I need to thank God for?

What did I realize that I need God's help with?

Write a prayer and let God know how you plan to apply these lessons and truths to your life:

In the Almighty Name of Jesus I pray, Amen

Date:

Who is the author or who is speaking in this verse?

Verse:

Did I learn anything that I can praise God for?

Did God tug at my heart about something I need to confess?

What did I realize that I need to thank God for?

What did I realize that I need God's help with?

Write a prayer and let God know how you plan to apply these lessons and truths to your life:

In the Almighty Name of Jesus I pray, Amen

Date:

Who is the author or who is speaking in this verse?

Verse:

Did I learn anything that I can praise God for?

Did God tug at my heart about something I need to confess?

What did I realize that I need to thank God for?

What did I realize that I need God's help with?

Write a prayer and let God know how you plan to apply these lessons
and truths to your life:

In the Almighty Name of Jesus I pray, Amen

Date:

Who is the author or who is speaking in this verse?

Verse:

Did I learn anything that I can praise God for?

Did God tug at my heart about something I need to confess?

What did I realize that I need to thank God for?

What did I realize that I need God's help with?

Write a prayer and let God know how you plan to apply these lessons
and truths to your life:

In the Almighty Name of Jesus I pray, Amen

Date:

Who is the author or who is speaking in this verse?

Verse:

Did I learn anything that I can praise God for?

Did God tug at my heart about something I need to confess?

What did I realize that I need to thank God for?

What did I realize that I need God's help with?

Write a prayer and let God know how you plan to apply these lessons
and truths to your life:

In the Almighty Name of Jesus I pray, Amen

Date:

Who is the author or who is speaking in this verse?

Verse:

Did I learn anything that I can praise God for?

Did God tug at my heart about something I need to confess?

What did I realize that I need to thank God for?

What did I realize that I need God's help with?

Write a prayer and let God know how you plan to apply these lessons
and truths to your life:

In the Almighty Name of Jesus I pray, Amen

Date:

Who is the author or who is speaking in this verse?

Verse:

Did I learn anything that I can praise God for?

Did God tug at my heart about something I need to confess?

What did I realize that I need to thank God for?

What did I realize that I need God's help with?

Write a prayer and let God know how you plan to apply these lessons
and truths to your life:

In the Almighty Name of Jesus I pray, Amen

Date:

Who is the author or who is speaking in this verse?

Verse:

Did I learn anything that I can praise God for?

Did God tug at my heart about something I need to confess?

What did I realize that I need to thank God for?

What did I realize that I need God's help with?

Write a prayer and let God know how you plan to apply these lessons and truths to your life:

In the Almighty Name of Jesus I pray, Amen

Date:

Who is the author or who is speaking in this verse?

Verse:

Did I learn anything that I can praise God for?

Did God tug at my heart about something I need to confess?

What did I realize that I need to thank God for?

What did I realize that I need God's help with?

Write a prayer and let God know how you plan to apply these lessons
and truths to your life:

In the Almighty Name of Jesus I pray, Amen

Date:

Who is the author or who is speaking in this verse?

Verse:

Did I learn anything that I can praise God for?

Did God tug at my heart about something I need to confess?

What did I realize that I need to thank God for?

What did I realize that I need God's help with?

Write a prayer and let God know how you plan to apply these lessons and truths to your life:

In the Almighty Name of Jesus I pray, Amen

Date:

Who is the author or who is speaking in this verse?

Verse:

Did I learn anything that I can praise God for?

Did God tug at my heart about something I need to confess?

What did I realize that I need to thank God for?

What did I realize that I need God's help with?

Write a prayer and let God know how you plan to apply these lessons and truths to your life:

In the Almighty Name of Jesus I pray, Amen

Date:

Who is the author or who is speaking in this verse?

Verse:

Did I learn anything that I can praise God for?

Did God tug at my heart about something I need to confess?

What did I realize that I need to thank God for?

What did I realize that I need God's help with?

Write a prayer and let God know how you plan to apply these lessons
and truths to your life:

In the Almighty Name of Jesus I pray, Amen

Date:

Who is the author or who is speaking in this verse?

Verse:

Did I learn anything that I can praise God for?

Did God tug at my heart about something I need to confess?

What did I realize that I need to thank God for?

What did I realize that I need God's help with?

Write a prayer and let God know how you plan to apply these lessons
and truths to your life:

In the Almighty Name of Jesus I pray, Amen

Date:

Who is the author or who is speaking in this verse?

Verse:

Did I learn anything that I can praise God for?

Did God tug at my heart about something I need to confess?

What did I realize that I need to thank God for?

What did I realize that I need God's help with?

Write a prayer and let God know how you plan to apply these lessons
and truths to your life:

In the Almighty Name of Jesus I pray, Amen

Date:

Who is the author or who is speaking in this verse?

Verse:

Did I learn anything that I can praise God for?

Did God tug at my heart about something I need to confess?

What did I realize that I need to thank God for?

What did I realize that I need God's help with?

Write a prayer and let God know how you plan to apply these lessons
and truths to your life:

In the Almighty Name of Jesus I pray, Amen

Date:

Who is the author or who is speaking in this verse?

Verse:

Did I learn anything that I can praise God for?

Did God tug at my heart about something I need to confess?

What did I realize that I need to thank God for?

What did I realize that I need God's help with?

Write a prayer and let God know how you plan to apply these lessons
and truths to your life:

In the Almighty Name of Jesus I pray, Amen

Date:

Who is the author or who is speaking in this verse?

Verse:

Did I learn anything that I can praise God for?

Did God tug at my heart about something I need to confess?

What did I realize that I need to thank God for?

What did I realize that I need God's help with?

Write a prayer and let God know how you plan to apply these lessons
and truths to your life:

In the Almighty Name of Jesus I pray, Amen

Date:

Who is the author or who is speaking in this verse?

Verse:

Did I learn anything that I can praise God for?

Did God tug at my heart about something I need to confess?

What did I realize that I need to thank God for?

What did I realize that I need God's help with?

Write a prayer and let God know how you plan to apply these lessons
and truths to your life:

In the Almighty Name of Jesus I pray, Amen

Date:

Who is the author or who is speaking in this verse?

Verse:

Did I learn anything that I can praise God for?

Did God tug at my heart about something I need to confess?

What did I realize that I need to thank God for?

What did I realize that I need God's help with?

Write a prayer and let God know how you plan to apply these lessons and truths to your life:

In the Almighty Name of Jesus I pray, Amen

Date:

Who is the author or who is speaking in this verse?

Verse:

Did I learn anything that I can praise God for?

Did God tug at my heart about something I need to confess?

What did I realize that I need to thank God for?

What did I realize that I need God's help with?

Write a prayer and let God know how you plan to apply these lessons and truths to your life:

In the Almighty Name of Jesus I pray, Amen

Date:

Who is the author or who is speaking in this verse?

Verse:

Did I learn anything that I can praise God for?

Did God tug at my heart about something I need to confess?

What did I realize that I need to thank God for?

What did I realize that I need God's help with?

Write a prayer and let God know how you plan to apply these lessons
and truths to your life:

In the Almighty Name of Jesus I pray, Amen

Date:

Who is the author or who is speaking in this verse?

Verse:

Did I learn anything that I can praise God for?

Did God tug at my heart about something I need to confess?

What did I realize that I need to thank God for?

What did I realize that I need God's help with?

Write a prayer and let God know how you plan to apply these lessons and truths to your life:

In the Almighty Name of Jesus I pray, Amen

Date:

Who is the author or who is speaking in this verse?

Verse:

Did I learn anything that I can praise God for?

Did God tug at my heart about something I need to confess?

What did I realize that I need to thank God for?

What did I realize that I need God's help with?

Write a prayer and let God know how you plan to apply these lessons
and truths to your life:

In the Almighty Name of Jesus I pray, Amen

Date:

Who is the author or who is speaking in this verse?

Verse:

Did I learn anything that I can praise God for?

Did God tug at my heart about something I need to confess?

What did I realize that I need to thank God for?

What did I realize that I need God's help with?

Write a prayer and let God know how you plan to apply these lessons
and truths to your life:

In the Almighty Name of Jesus I pray, Amen

Date:

Who is the author or who is speaking in this verse?

Verse:

Did I learn anything that I can praise God for?

Did God tug at my heart about something I need to confess?

What did I realize that I need to thank God for?

What did I realize that I need God's help with?

Write a prayer and let God know how you plan to apply these lessons
and truths to your life:

In the Almighty Name of Jesus I pray, Amen

Date:

Who is the author or who is speaking in this verse?

Verse:

Did I learn anything that I can praise God for?

Did God tug at my heart about something I need to confess?

What did I realize that I need to thank God for?

What did I realize that I need God's help with?

Write a prayer and let God know how you plan to apply these lessons and truths to your life:

In the Almighty Name of Jesus I pray, Amen

Date:

Who is the author or who is speaking in this verse?

Verse:

Did I learn anything that I can praise God for?

Did God tug at my heart about something I need to confess?

What did I realize that I need to thank God for?

What did I realize that I need God's help with?

Write a prayer and let God know how you plan to apply these lessons and truths to your life:

In the Almighty Name of Jesus I pray, Amen

Date:

Who is the author or who is speaking in this verse?

Verse:

Did I learn anything that I can praise God for?

Did God tug at my heart about something I need to confess?

What did I realize that I need to thank God for?

What did I realize that I need God's help with?

Write a prayer and let God know how you plan to apply these lessons
and truths to your life:

In the Almighty Name of Jesus I pray, Amen

Date:

Who is the author or who is speaking in this verse?

Verse:

Did I learn anything that I can praise God for?

Did God tug at my heart about something I need to confess?

What did I realize that I need to thank God for?

What did I realize that I need God's help with?

Write a prayer and let God know how you plan to apply these lessons and truths to your life:

In the Almighty Name of Jesus I pray, Amen

Date:

Who is the author or who is speaking in this verse?

Verse:

Did I learn anything that I can praise God for?

Did God tug at my heart about something I need to confess?

What did I realize that I need to thank God for?

What did I realize that I need God's help with?

Write a prayer and let God know how you plan to apply these lessons
and truths to your life:

In the Almighty Name of Jesus I pray, Amen

Date:

Who is the author or who is speaking in this verse?

Verse:

Did I learn anything that I can praise God for?

Did God tug at my heart about something I need to confess?

What did I realize that I need to thank God for?

What did I realize that I need God's help with?

Write a prayer and let God know how you plan to apply these lessons
and truths to your life:

In the Almighty Name of Jesus I pray, Amen

Date:

Who is the author or who is speaking in this verse?

Verse:

Did I learn anything that I can praise God for?

Did God tug at my heart about something I need to confess?

What did I realize that I need to thank God for?

What did I realize that I need God's help with?

Write a prayer and let God know how you plan to apply these lessons and truths to your life:

In the Almighty Name of Jesus I pray, Amen

Date:

Who is the author or who is speaking in this verse?

Verse:

Did I learn anything that I can praise God for?

Did God tug at my heart about something I need to confess?

What did I realize that I need to thank God for?

What did I realize that I need God's help with?

Write a prayer and let God know how you plan to apply these lessons and truths to your life:

In the Almighty Name of Jesus I pray, Amen

Date:

Who is the author or who is speaking in this verse?

Verse:

Did I learn anything that I can praise God for?

Did God tug at my heart about something I need to confess?

What did I realize that I need to thank God for?

What did I realize that I need God's help with?

Write a prayer and let God know how you plan to apply these lessons and truths to your life:

In the Almighty Name of Jesus I pray, Amen

Date:

Who is the author or who is speaking in this verse?

Verse:

Did I learn anything that I can praise God for?

Did God tug at my heart about something I need to confess?

What did I realize that I need to thank God for?

What did I realize that I need God's help with?

Write a prayer and let God know how you plan to apply these lessons and truths to your life:

In the Almighty Name of Jesus I pray, Amen

Date:

Who is the author or who is speaking in this verse?

Verse:

Did I learn anything that I can praise God for?

Did God tug at my heart about something I need to confess?

What did I realize that I need to thank God for?

What did I realize that I need God's help with?

Write a prayer and let God know how you plan to apply these lessons
and truths to your life:

In the Almighty Name of Jesus I pray, Amen

Date:

Who is the author or who is speaking in this verse?

Verse:

Did I learn anything that I can praise God for?

Did God tug at my heart about something I need to confess?

What did I realize that I need to thank God for?

What did I realize that I need God's help with?

Write a prayer and let God know how you plan to apply these lessons and truths to your life:

In the Almighty Name of Jesus I pray, Amen

Date:

Who is the author or who is speaking in this verse?

Verse:

Did I learn anything that I can praise God for?

Did God tug at my heart about something I need to confess?

What did I realize that I need to thank God for?

What did I realize that I need God's help with?

Write a prayer and let God know how you plan to apply these lessons and truths to your life:

In the Almighty Name of Jesus I pray, Amen

Date:

Who is the author or who is speaking in this verse?

Verse:

Did I learn anything that I can praise God for?

Did God tug at my heart about something I need to confess?

What did I realize that I need to thank God for?

What did I realize that I need God's help with?

Write a prayer and let God know how you plan to apply these lessons and truths to your life:

In the Almighty Name of Jesus I pray, Amen

Date:

Who is the author or who is speaking in this verse?

Verse:

Did I learn anything that I can praise God for?

Did God tug at my heart about something I need to confess?

What did I realize that I need to thank God for?

What did I realize that I need God's help with?

Write a prayer and let God know how you plan to apply these lessons
and truths to your life:

In the Almighty Name of Jesus I pray, Amen

Date:

Who is the author or who is speaking in this verse?

Verse:

Did I learn anything that I can praise God for?

Did God tug at my heart about something I need to confess?

What did I realize that I need to thank God for?

What did I realize that I need God's help with?

Write a prayer and let God know how you plan to apply these lessons and truths to your life:

In the Almighty Name of Jesus I pray, Amen

Date:

Who is the author or who is speaking in this verse?

Verse:

Did I learn anything that I can praise God for?

Did God tug at my heart about something I need to confess?

What did I realize that I need to thank God for?

What did I realize that I need God's help with?

Write a prayer and let God know how you plan to apply these lessons
and truths to your life:

In the Almighty Name of Jesus I pray, Amen

Date:

Who is the author or who is speaking in this verse?

Verse:

Did I learn anything that I can praise God for?

Did God tug at my heart about something I need to confess?

What did I realize that I need to thank God for?

What did I realize that I need God's help with?

Write a prayer and let God know how you plan to apply these lessons
and truths to your life:

In the Almighty Name of Jesus I pray, Amen

Date:

Who is the author or who is speaking in this verse?

Verse:

Did I learn anything that I can praise God for?

Did God tug at my heart about something I need to confess?

What did I realize that I need to thank God for?

What did I realize that I need God's help with?

Write a prayer and let God know how you plan to apply these lessons and truths to your life:

In the Almighty Name of Jesus I pray, Amen

Date:

Who is the author or who is speaking in this verse?

Verse:

Did I learn anything that I can praise God for?

Did God tug at my heart about something I need to confess?

What did I realize that I need to thank God for?

What did I realize that I need God's help with?

Write a prayer and let God know how you plan to apply these lessons and truths to your life:

In the Almighty Name of Jesus I pray, Amen

Date:

Who is the author or who is speaking in this verse?

Verse:

Did I learn anything that I can praise God for?

Did God tug at my heart about something I need to confess?

What did I realize that I need to thank God for?

What did I realize that I need God's help with?

Write a prayer and let God know how you plan to apply these lessons
and truths to your life:

In the Almighty Name of Jesus I pray, Amen

Date:

Who is the author or who is speaking in this verse?

Verse:

Did I learn anything that I can praise God for?

Did God tug at my heart about something I need to confess?

What did I realize that I need to thank God for?

What did I realize that I need God's help with?

Write a prayer and let God know how you plan to apply these lessons and truths to your life:

In the Almighty Name of Jesus I pray, Amen

Date:

Who is the author or who is speaking in this verse?

Verse:

Did I learn anything that I can praise God for?

Did God tug at my heart about something I need to confess?

What did I realize that I need to thank God for?

What did I realize that I need God's help with?

Write a prayer and let God know how you plan to apply these lessons
and truths to your life:

In the Almighty Name of Jesus I pray, Amen

Date:

Who is the author or who is speaking in this verse?

Verse:

Did I learn anything that I can praise God for?

Did God tug at my heart about something I need to confess?

What did I realize that I need to thank God for?

What did I realize that I need God's help with?

Write a prayer and let God know how you plan to apply these lessons and truths to your life:

In the Almighty Name of Jesus I pray, Amen

Date:

Who is the author or who is speaking in this verse?

Verse:

Did I learn anything that I can praise God for?

Did God tug at my heart about something I need to confess?

What did I realize that I need to thank God for?

What did I realize that I need God's help with?

Write a prayer and let God know how you plan to apply these lessons and truths to your life:

In the Almighty Name of Jesus I pray, Amen

Date:

Who is the author or who is speaking in this verse?

Verse:

Did I learn anything that I can praise God for?

Did God tug at my heart about something I need to confess?

What did I realize that I need to thank God for?

What did I realize that I need God's help with?

Write a prayer and let God know how you plan to apply these lessons and truths to your life:

In the Almighty Name of Jesus I pray, Amen

Date:

Who is the author or who is speaking in this verse?

Verse:

Did I learn anything that I can praise God for?

Did God tug at my heart about something I need to confess?

What did I realize that I need to thank God for?

What did I realize that I need God's help with?

Write a prayer and let God know how you plan to apply these lessons and truths to your life:

In the Almighty Name of Jesus I pray, Amen

Date:

Who is the author or who is speaking in this verse?

Verse:

Did I learn anything that I can praise God for?

Did God tug at my heart about something I need to confess?

What did I realize that I need to thank God for?

What did I realize that I need God's help with?

Write a prayer and let God know how you plan to apply these lessons
and truths to your life:

In the Almighty Name of Jesus I pray, Amen

Date:

Who is the author or who is speaking in this verse?

Verse:

Did I learn anything that I can praise God for?

Did God tug at my heart about something I need to confess?

What did I realize that I need to thank God for?

What did I realize that I need God's help with?

Write a prayer and let God know how you plan to apply these lessons
and truths to your life:

In the Almighty Name of Jesus I pray, Amen

Date:

Who is the author or who is speaking in this verse?

Verse:

Did I learn anything that I can praise God for?

Did God tug at my heart about something I need to confess?

What did I realize that I need to thank God for?

What did I realize that I need God's help with?

Write a prayer and let God know how you plan to apply these lessons
and truths to your life:

In the Almighty Name of Jesus I pray, Amen

Date:

Who is the author or who is speaking in this verse?

Verse:

Did I learn anything that I can praise God for?

Did God tug at my heart about something I need to confess?

What did I realize that I need to thank God for?

What did I realize that I need God's help with?

Write a prayer and let God know how you plan to apply these lessons
and truths to your life:

In the Almighty Name of Jesus I pray, Amen

Date:

Who is the author or who is speaking in this verse?

Verse:

Did I learn anything that I can praise God for?

Did God tug at my heart about something I need to confess?

What did I realize that I need to thank God for?

What did I realize that I need God's help with?

Write a prayer and let God know how you plan to apply these lessons and truths to your life:

In the Almighty Name of Jesus I pray, Amen

Date:

Who is the author or who is speaking in this verse?

Verse:

Did I learn anything that I can praise God for?

Did God tug at my heart about something I need to confess?

What did I realize that I need to thank God for?

What did I realize that I need God's help with?

Write a prayer and let God know how you plan to apply these lessons and truths to your life:

In the Almighty Name of Jesus I pray, Amen

Date:

Who is the author or who is speaking in this verse?

Verse:

Did I learn anything that I can praise God for?

Did God tug at my heart about something I need to confess?

What did I realize that I need to thank God for?

What did I realize that I need God's help with?

Write a prayer and let God know how you plan to apply these lessons
and truths to your life:

In the Almighty Name of Jesus I pray, Amen

Date:

Who is the author or who is speaking in this verse?

Verse:

Did I learn anything that I can praise God for?

Did God tug at my heart about something I need to confess?

What did I realize that I need to thank God for?

What did I realize that I need God's help with?

Write a prayer and let God know how you plan to apply these lessons and truths to your life:

In the Almighty Name of Jesus I pray, Amen

Date:

Who is the author or who is speaking in this verse?

Verse:

Did I learn anything that I can praise God for?

Did God tug at my heart about something I need to confess?

What did I realize that I need to thank God for?

What did I realize that I need God's help with?

Write a prayer and let God know how you plan to apply these lessons and truths to your life:

In the Almighty Name of Jesus I pray, Amen

Date:

Who is the author or who is speaking in this verse?

Verse:

Did I learn anything that I can praise God for?

Did God tug at my heart about something I need to confess?

What did I realize that I need to thank God for?

What did I realize that I need God's help with?

Write a prayer and let God know how you plan to apply these lessons and truths to your life:

In the Almighty Name of Jesus I pray, Amen

Date:

Who is the author or who is speaking in this verse?

Verse:

Did I learn anything that I can praise God for?

Did God tug at my heart about something I need to confess?

What did I realize that I need to thank God for?

What did I realize that I need God's help with?

Write a prayer and let God know how you plan to apply these lessons
and truths to your life:

In the Almighty Name of Jesus I pray, Amen

Date:

Who is the author or who is speaking in this verse?

Verse:

Did I learn anything that I can praise God for?

Did God tug at my heart about something I need to confess?

What did I realize that I need to thank God for?

What did I realize that I need God's help with?

Write a prayer and let God know how you plan to apply these lessons and truths to your life:

In the Almighty Name of Jesus I pray, Amen

Date:

Who is the author or who is speaking in this verse?

Verse:

Did I learn anything that I can praise God for?

Did God tug at my heart about something I need to confess?

What did I realize that I need to thank God for?

What did I realize that I need God's help with?

Write a prayer and let God know how you plan to apply these lessons and truths to your life:

In the Almighty Name of Jesus I pray, Amen

Date:

Who is the author or who is speaking in this verse?

Verse:

Did I learn anything that I can praise God for?

Did God tug at my heart about something I need to confess?

What did I realize that I need to thank God for?

What did I realize that I need God's help with?

Write a prayer and let God know how you plan to apply these lessons
and truths to your life:

In the Almighty Name of Jesus I pray, Amen

Date:

Who is the author or who is speaking in this verse?

Verse:

Did I learn anything that I can praise God for?

Did God tug at my heart about something I need to confess?

What did I realize that I need to thank God for?

What did I realize that I need God's help with?

Write a prayer and let God know how you plan to apply these lessons
and truths to your life:

In the Almighty Name of Jesus I pray, Amen

Date:

Who is the author or who is speaking in this verse?

Verse:

Did I learn anything that I can praise God for?

Did God tug at my heart about something I need to confess?

What did I realize that I need to thank God for?

What did I realize that I need God's help with?

Write a prayer and let God know how you plan to apply these lessons
and truths to your life:

In the Almighty Name of Jesus I pray, Amen

Date:

Who is the author or who is speaking in this verse?

Verse:

Did I learn anything that I can praise God for?

Did God tug at my heart about something I need to confess?

What did I realize that I need to thank God for?

What did I realize that I need God's help with?

Write a prayer and let God know how you plan to apply these lessons and truths to your life:

In the Almighty Name of Jesus I pray, Amen

Date:

Who is the author or who is speaking in this verse?

Verse:

Did I learn anything that I can praise God for?

Did God tug at my heart about something I need to confess?

What did I realize that I need to thank God for?

What did I realize that I need God's help with?

Write a prayer and let God know how you plan to apply these lessons
and truths to your life:

In the Almighty Name of Jesus I pray, Amen

Date:

Who is the author or who is speaking in this verse?

Verse:

Did I learn anything that I can praise God for?

Did God tug at my heart about something I need to confess?

What did I realize that I need to thank God for?

What did I realize that I need God's help with?

Write a prayer and let God know how you plan to apply these lessons
and truths to your life:

In the Almighty Name of Jesus I pray, Amen

Date:

Who is the author or who is speaking in this verse?

Verse:

Did I learn anything that I can praise God for?

Did God tug at my heart about something I need to confess?

What did I realize that I need to thank God for?

What did I realize that I need God's help with?

Write a prayer and let God know how you plan to apply these lessons and truths to your life:

In the Almighty Name of Jesus I pray, Amen

Date:

Who is the author or who is speaking in this verse?

Verse:

Did I learn anything that I can praise God for?

Did God tug at my heart about something I need to confess?

What did I realize that I need to thank God for?

What did I realize that I need God's help with?

Write a prayer and let God know how you plan to apply these lessons and truths to your life:

In the Almighty Name of Jesus I pray, Amen

Date:

Who is the author or who is speaking in this verse?

Verse:

Did I learn anything that I can praise God for?

Did God tug at my heart about something I need to confess?

What did I realize that I need to thank God for?

What did I realize that I need God's help with?

Write a prayer and let God know how you plan to apply these lessons and truths to your life:

In the Almighty Name of Jesus I pray, Amen

Date:

Who is the author or who is speaking in this verse?

Verse:

Did I learn anything that I can praise God for?

Did God tug at my heart about something I need to confess?

What did I realize that I need to thank God for?

What did I realize that I need God's help with?

Write a prayer and let God know how you plan to apply these lessons
and truths to your life:

In the Almighty Name of Jesus I pray, Amen

Date:

Who is the author or who is speaking in this verse?

Verse:

Did I learn anything that I can praise God for?

Did God tug at my heart about something I need to confess?

What did I realize that I need to thank God for?

What did I realize that I need God's help with?

Write a prayer and let God know how you plan to apply these lessons
and truths to your life:

In the Almighty Name of Jesus I pray, Amen

Date:

Who is the author or who is speaking in this verse?

Verse:

Did I learn anything that I can praise God for?

Did God tug at my heart about something I need to confess?

What did I realize that I need to thank God for?

What did I realize that I need God's help with?

Write a prayer and let God know how you plan to apply these lessons
and truths to your life:

In the Almighty Name of Jesus I pray, Amen

Date:

Who is the author or who is speaking in this verse?

Verse:

Did I learn anything that I can praise God for?

Did God tug at my heart about something I need to confess?

What did I realize that I need to thank God for?

What did I realize that I need God's help with?

Write a prayer and let God know how you plan to apply these lessons
and truths to your life:

In the Almighty Name of Jesus I pray, Amen

Date:

Who is the author or who is speaking in this verse?

Verse:

Did I learn anything that I can praise God for?

Did God tug at my heart about something I need to confess?

What did I realize that I need to thank God for?

What did I realize that I need God's help with?

Write a prayer and let God know how you plan to apply these lessons
and truths to your life:

In the Almighty Name of Jesus I pray, Amen

Date:

Who is the author or who is speaking in this verse?

Verse:

Did I learn anything that I can praise God for?

Did God tug at my heart about something I need to confess?

What did I realize that I need to thank God for?

What did I realize that I need God's help with?

Write a prayer and let God know how you plan to apply these lessons and truths to your life:

In the Almighty Name of Jesus I pray, Amen

Date:

Who is the author or who is speaking in this verse?

Verse:

Did I learn anything that I can praise God for?

Did God tug at my heart about something I need to confess?

What did I realize that I need to thank God for?

What did I realize that I need God's help with?

Write a prayer and let God know how you plan to apply these lessons
and truths to your life:

In the Almighty Name of Jesus I pray, Amen

Date:

Who is the author or who is speaking in this verse?

Verse:

Did I learn anything that I can praise God for?

Did God tug at my heart about something I need to confess?

What did I realize that I need to thank God for?

What did I realize that I need God's help with?

Write a prayer and let God know how you plan to apply these lessons
and truths to your life:

In the Almighty Name of Jesus I pray, Amen

Date:

Who is the author or who is speaking in this verse?

Verse:

Did I learn anything that I can praise God for?

Did God tug at my heart about something I need to confess?

What did I realize that I need to thank God for?

What did I realize that I need God's help with?

Write a prayer and let God know how you plan to apply these lessons
and truths to your life:

In the Almighty Name of Jesus I pray, Amen

Date:

Who is the author or who is speaking in this verse?

Verse:

Did I learn anything that I can praise God for?

Did God tug at my heart about something I need to confess?

What did I realize that I need to thank God for?

What did I realize that I need God's help with?

Write a prayer and let God know how you plan to apply these lessons
and truths to your life:

In the Almighty Name of Jesus I pray, Amen

Date:

Who is the author or who is speaking in this verse?

Verse:

Did I learn anything that I can praise God for?

Did God tug at my heart about something I need to confess?

What did I realize that I need to thank God for?

What did I realize that I need God's help with?

Write a prayer and let God know how you plan to apply these lessons
and truths to your life:

In the Almighty Name of Jesus I pray, Amen

Date:

Who is the author or who is speaking in this verse?

Verse:

Did I learn anything that I can praise God for?

Did God tug at my heart about something I need to confess?

What did I realize that I need to thank God for?

What did I realize that I need God's help with?

Write a prayer and let God know how you plan to apply these lessons
and truths to your life:

In the Almighty Name of Jesus I pray, Amen

Date:

Who is the author or who is speaking in this verse?

Verse:

Did I learn anything that I can praise God for?

Did God tug at my heart about something I need to confess?

What did I realize that I need to thank God for?

What did I realize that I need God's help with?

Write a prayer and let God know how you plan to apply these lessons
and truths to your life:

In the Almighty Name of Jesus I pray, Amen

Date:

Who is the author or who is speaking in this verse?

Verse:

Did I learn anything that I can praise God for?

Did God tug at my heart about something I need to confess?

What did I realize that I need to thank God for?

What did I realize that I need God's help with?

Write a prayer and let God know how you plan to apply these lessons
and truths to your life:

In the Almighty Name of Jesus I pray, Amen

Date:

Who is the author or who is speaking in this verse?

Verse:

Did I learn anything that I can praise God for?

Did God tug at my heart about something I need to confess?

What did I realize that I need to thank God for?

What did I realize that I need God's help with?

Write a prayer and let God know how you plan to apply these lessons
and truths to your life:

In the Almighty Name of Jesus I pray, Amen

Date:

Who is the author or who is speaking in this verse?

Verse:

Did I learn anything that I can praise God for?

Did God tug at my heart about something I need to confess?

What did I realize that I need to thank God for?

What did I realize that I need God's help with?

Write a prayer and let God know how you plan to apply these lessons and truths to your life:

In the Almighty Name of Jesus I pray, Amen

Date:

Who is the author or who is speaking in this verse?

Verse:

Did I learn anything that I can praise God for?

Did God tug at my heart about something I need to confess?

What did I realize that I need to thank God for?

What did I realize that I need God's help with?

Write a prayer and let God know how you plan to apply these lessons and truths to your life:

In the Almighty Name of Jesus I pray, Amen

Date:

Who is the author or who is speaking in this verse?

Verse:

Did I learn anything that I can praise God for?

Did God tug at my heart about something I need to confess?

What did I realize that I need to thank God for?

What did I realize that I need God's help with?

Write a prayer and let God know how you plan to apply these lessons and truths to your life:

In the Almighty Name of Jesus I pray, Amen

Date:

Who is the author or who is speaking in this verse?

Verse:

Did I learn anything that I can praise God for?

Did God tug at my heart about something I need to confess?

What did I realize that I need to thank God for?

What did I realize that I need God's help with?

Write a prayer and let God know how you plan to apply these lessons and truths to your life:

In the Almighty Name of Jesus I pray, Amen

Date:

Who is the author or who is speaking in this verse?

Verse:

Did I learn anything that I can praise God for?

Did God tug at my heart about something I need to confess?

What did I realize that I need to thank God for?

What did I realize that I need God's help with?

Write a prayer and let God know how you plan to apply these lessons
and truths to your life:

In the Almighty Name of Jesus I pray, Amen

Date:

Who is the author or who is speaking in this verse?

Verse:

Did I learn anything that I can praise God for?

Did God tug at my heart about something I need to confess?

What did I realize that I need to thank God for?

What did I realize that I need God's help with?

Write a prayer and let God know how you plan to apply these lessons
and truths to your life:

In the Almighty Name of Jesus I pray, Amen

Date:

Who is the author or who is speaking in this verse?

Verse:

Did I learn anything that I can praise God for?

Did God tug at my heart about something I need to confess?

What did I realize that I need to thank God for?

What did I realize that I need God's help with?

Write a prayer and let God know how you plan to apply these lessons and truths to your life:

In the Almighty Name of Jesus I pray, Amen

Date:

Who is the author or who is speaking in this verse?

Verse:

Did I learn anything that I can praise God for?

Did God tug at my heart about something I need to confess?

What did I realize that I need to thank God for?

What did I realize that I need God's help with?

Write a prayer and let God know how you plan to apply these lessons
and truths to your life:

In the Almighty Name of Jesus I pray, Amen

Date:

Who is the author or who is speaking in this verse?

Verse:

Did I learn anything that I can praise God for?

Did God tug at my heart about something I need to confess?

What did I realize that I need to thank God for?

What did I realize that I need God's help with?

Write a prayer and let God know how you plan to apply these lessons
and truths to your life:

In the Almighty Name of Jesus I pray, Amen

Date:

Who is the author or who is speaking in this verse?

Verse:

Did I learn anything that I can praise God for?

Did God tug at my heart about something I need to confess?

What did I realize that I need to thank God for?

What did I realize that I need God's help with?

Write a prayer and let God know how you plan to apply these lessons and truths to your life:

In the Almighty Name of Jesus I pray, Amen

Date:

Who is the author or who is speaking in this verse?

Verse:

Did I learn anything that I can praise God for?

Did God tug at my heart about something I need to confess?

What did I realize that I need to thank God for?

What did I realize that I need God's help with?

Write a prayer and let God know how you plan to apply these lessons
and truths to your life:

In the Almighty Name of Jesus I pray, Amen

Date:

Who is the author or who is speaking in this verse?

Verse:

Did I learn anything that I can praise God for?

Did God tug at my heart about something I need to confess?

What did I realize that I need to thank God for?

What did I realize that I need God's help with?

Write a prayer and let God know how you plan to apply these lessons
and truths to your life:

In the Almighty Name of Jesus I pray, Amen

Date:

Who is the author or who is speaking in this verse?

Verse:

Did I learn anything that I can praise God for?

Did God tug at my heart about something I need to confess?

What did I realize that I need to thank God for?

What did I realize that I need God's help with?

Write a prayer and let God know how you plan to apply these lessons
and truths to your life:

In the Almighty Name of Jesus I pray, Amen

Date:

Who is the author or who is speaking in this verse?

Verse:

Did I learn anything that I can praise God for?

Did God tug at my heart about something I need to confess?

What did I realize that I need to thank God for?

What did I realize that I need God's help with?

Write a prayer and let God know how you plan to apply these lessons
and truths to your life:

In the Almighty Name of Jesus I pray, Amen

Date:

Who is the author or who is speaking in this verse?

Verse:

Did I learn anything that I can praise God for?

Did God tug at my heart about something I need to confess?

What did I realize that I need to thank God for?

What did I realize that I need God's help with?

Write a prayer and let God know how you plan to apply these lessons
and truths to your life:

In the Almighty Name of Jesus I pray, Amen

Date:

Who is the author or who is speaking in this verse?

Verse:

Did I learn anything that I can praise God for?

Did God tug at my heart about something I need to confess?

What did I realize that I need to thank God for?

What did I realize that I need God's help with?

Write a prayer and let God know how you plan to apply these lessons
and truths to your life:

In the Almighty Name of Jesus I pray, Amen

Date:

Who is the author or who is speaking in this verse?

Verse:

Did I learn anything that I can praise God for?

Did God tug at my heart about something I need to confess?

What did I realize that I need to thank God for?

What did I realize that I need God's help with?

Write a prayer and let God know how you plan to apply these lessons
and truths to your life:

In the Almighty Name of Jesus I pray, Amen

Date:

Who is the author or who is speaking in this verse?

Verse:

Did I learn anything that I can praise God for?

Did God tug at my heart about something I need to confess?

What did I realize that I need to thank God for?

What did I realize that I need God's help with?

Write a prayer and let God know how you plan to apply these lessons
and truths to your life:

In the Almighty Name of Jesus I pray, Amen

Date:

Who is the author or who is speaking in this verse?

Verse:

Did I learn anything that I can praise God for?

Did God tug at my heart about something I need to confess?

What did I realize that I need to thank God for?

What did I realize that I need God's help with?

Write a prayer and let God know how you plan to apply these lessons and truths to your life:

In the Almighty Name of Jesus I pray, Amen

Date:

Who is the author or who is speaking in this verse?

Verse:

Did I learn anything that I can praise God for?

Did God tug at my heart about something I need to confess?

What did I realize that I need to thank God for?

What did I realize that I need God's help with?

Write a prayer and let God know how you plan to apply these lessons
and truths to your life:

In the Almighty Name of Jesus I pray, Amen

Date:

Who is the author or who is speaking in this verse?

Verse:

Did I learn anything that I can praise God for?

Did God tug at my heart about something I need to confess?

What did I realize that I need to thank God for?

What did I realize that I need God's help with?

Write a prayer and let God know how you plan to apply these lessons
and truths to your life:

In the Almighty Name of Jesus I pray, Amen

Date:

Who is the author or who is speaking in this verse?

Verse:

Did I learn anything that I can praise God for?

Did God tug at my heart about something I need to confess?

What did I realize that I need to thank God for?

What did I realize that I need God's help with?

Write a prayer and let God know how you plan to apply these lessons and truths to your life:

In the Almighty Name of Jesus I pray, Amen

Date:

Who is the author or who is speaking in this verse?

Verse:

Did I learn anything that I can praise God for?

Did God tug at my heart about something I need to confess?

What did I realize that I need to thank God for?

What did I realize that I need God's help with?

Write a prayer and let God know how you plan to apply these lessons and truths to your life:

In the Almighty Name of Jesus I pray, Amen

Date:

Who is the author or who is speaking in this verse?

Verse:

Did I learn anything that I can praise God for?

Did God tug at my heart about something I need to confess?

What did I realize that I need to thank God for?

What did I realize that I need God's help with?

Write a prayer and let God know how you plan to apply these lessons and truths to your life:

In the Almighty Name of Jesus I pray, Amen

Date:

Who is the author or who is speaking in this verse?

Verse:

Did I learn anything that I can praise God for?

Did God tug at my heart about something I need to confess?

What did I realize that I need to thank God for?

What did I realize that I need God's help with?

Write a prayer and let God know how you plan to apply these lessons and truths to your life:

In the Almighty Name of Jesus I pray, Amen

Date:

Who is the author or who is speaking in this verse?

Verse:

Did I learn anything that I can praise God for?

Did God tug at my heart about something I need to confess?

What did I realize that I need to thank God for?

What did I realize that I need God's help with?

Write a prayer and let God know how you plan to apply these lessons
and truths to your life:

In the Almighty Name of Jesus I pray, Amen

Date:

Who is the author or who is speaking in this verse?

Verse:

Did I learn anything that I can praise God for?

Did God tug at my heart about something I need to confess?

What did I realize that I need to thank God for?

What did I realize that I need God's help with?

Write a prayer and let God know how you plan to apply these lessons and truths to your life:

In the Almighty Name of Jesus I pray, Amen

Date:

Who is the author or who is speaking in this verse?

Verse:

Did I learn anything that I can praise God for?

Did God tug at my heart about something I need to confess?

What did I realize that I need to thank God for?

What did I realize that I need God's help with?

Write a prayer and let God know how you plan to apply these lessons and truths to your life:

In the Almighty Name of Jesus I pray, Amen

Date:

Who is the author or who is speaking in this verse?

Verse:

Did I learn anything that I can praise God for?

Did God tug at my heart about something I need to confess?

What did I realize that I need to thank God for?

What did I realize that I need God's help with?

Write a prayer and let God know how you plan to apply these lessons and truths to your life:

In the Almighty Name of Jesus I pray, Amen

Date:

Who is the author or who is speaking in this verse?

Verse:

Did I learn anything that I can praise God for?

Did God tug at my heart about something I need to confess?

What did I realize that I need to thank God for?

What did I realize that I need God's help with?

Write a prayer and let God know how you plan to apply these lessons and truths to your life:

In the Almighty Name of Jesus I pray, Amen

Date:

Who is the author or who is speaking in this verse?

Verse:

Did I learn anything that I can praise God for?

Did God tug at my heart about something I need to confess?

What did I realize that I need to thank God for?

What did I realize that I need God's help with?

Write a prayer and let God know how you plan to apply these lessons
and truths to your life:

In the Almighty Name of Jesus I pray, Amen

Date:

Who is the author or who is speaking in this verse?

Verse:

Did I learn anything that I can praise God for?

Did God tug at my heart about something I need to confess?

What did I realize that I need to thank God for?

What did I realize that I need God's help with?

Write a prayer and let God know how you plan to apply these lessons
and truths to your life:

In the Almighty Name of Jesus I pray, Amen

Date:

Who is the author or who is speaking in this verse?

Verse:

Did I learn anything that I can praise God for?

Did God tug at my heart about something I need to confess?

What did I realize that I need to thank God for?

What did I realize that I need God's help with?

Write a prayer and let God know how you plan to apply these lessons
and truths to your life:

In the Almighty Name of Jesus I pray, Amen

Date:

Who is the author or who is speaking in this verse?

Verse:

Did I learn anything that I can praise God for?

Did God tug at my heart about something I need to confess?

What did I realize that I need to thank God for?

What did I realize that I need God's help with?

Write a prayer and let God know how you plan to apply these lessons
and truths to your life:

In the Almighty Name of Jesus I pray, Amen

Date:

Who is the author or who is speaking in this verse?

Verse:

Did I learn anything that I can praise God for?

Did God tug at my heart about something I need to confess?

What did I realize that I need to thank God for?

What did I realize that I need God's help with?

Write a prayer and let God know how you plan to apply these lessons
and truths to your life:

In the Almighty Name of Jesus I pray, Amen

Date:

Who is the author or who is speaking in this verse?

Verse:

Did I learn anything that I can praise God for?

Did God tug at my heart about something I need to confess?

What did I realize that I need to thank God for?

What did I realize that I need God's help with?

Write a prayer and let God know how you plan to apply these lessons
and truths to your life:

In the Almighty Name of Jesus I pray, Amen

Date:

Who is the author or who is speaking in this verse?

Verse:

Did I learn anything that I can praise God for?

Did God tug at my heart about something I need to confess?

What did I realize that I need to thank God for?

What did I realize that I need God's help with?

Write a prayer and let God know how you plan to apply these lessons
and truths to your life:

In the Almighty Name of Jesus I pray, Amen

Date:

Who is the author or who is speaking in this verse?

Verse:

Did I learn anything that I can praise God for?

Did God tug at my heart about something I need to confess?

What did I realize that I need to thank God for?

What did I realize that I need God's help with?

Write a prayer and let God know how you plan to apply these lessons and truths to your life:

In the Almighty Name of Jesus I pray, Amen

Date:

Who is the author or who is speaking in this verse?

Verse:

Did I learn anything that I can praise God for?

Did God tug at my heart about something I need to confess?

What did I realize that I need to thank God for?

What did I realize that I need God's help with?

Write a prayer and let God know how you plan to apply these lessons
and truths to your life:

In the Almighty Name of Jesus I pray, Amen

Date:

Who is the author or who is speaking in this verse?

Verse:

Did I learn anything that I can praise God for?

Did God tug at my heart about something I need to confess?

What did I realize that I need to thank God for?

What did I realize that I need God's help with?

Write a prayer and let God know how you plan to apply these lessons
and truths to your life:

In the Almighty Name of Jesus I pray, Amen

Date:

Who is the author or who is speaking in this verse?

Verse:

Did I learn anything that I can praise God for?

Did God tug at my heart about something I need to confess?

What did I realize that I need to thank God for?

What did I realize that I need God's help with?

Write a prayer and let God know how you plan to apply these lessons
and truths to your life:

In the Almighty Name of Jesus I pray, Amen

Date:

Who is the author or who is speaking in this verse?

Verse:

Did I learn anything that I can praise God for?

Did God tug at my heart about something I need to confess?

What did I realize that I need to thank God for?

What did I realize that I need God's help with?

Write a prayer and let God know how you plan to apply these lessons
and truths to your life:

In the Almighty Name of Jesus I pray, Amen

Date:

Who is the author or who is speaking in this verse?

Verse:

Did I learn anything that I can praise God for?

Did God tug at my heart about something I need to confess?

What did I realize that I need to thank God for?

What did I realize that I need God's help with?

Write a prayer and let God know how you plan to apply these lessons and truths to your life:

In the Almighty Name of Jesus I pray, Amen

Date:

Who is the author or who is speaking in this verse?

Verse:

Did I learn anything that I can praise God for?

Did God tug at my heart about something I need to confess?

What did I realize that I need to thank God for?

What did I realize that I need God's help with?

Write a prayer and let God know how you plan to apply these lessons and truths to your life:

In the Almighty Name of Jesus I pray, Amen

Date:

Who is the author or who is speaking in this verse?

Verse:

Did I learn anything that I can praise God for?

Did God tug at my heart about something I need to confess?

What did I realize that I need to thank God for?

What did I realize that I need God's help with?

Write a prayer and let God know how you plan to apply these lessons
and truths to your life:

In the Almighty Name of Jesus I pray, Amen

Date:

Who is the author or who is speaking in this verse?

Verse:

Did I learn anything that I can praise God for?

Did God tug at my heart about something I need to confess?

What did I realize that I need to thank God for?

What did I realize that I need God's help with?

Write a prayer and let God know how you plan to apply these lessons
and truths to your life:

In the Almighty Name of Jesus I pray, Amen

Date:

Who is the author or who is speaking in this verse?

Verse:

Did I learn anything that I can praise God for?

Did God tug at my heart about something I need to confess?

What did I realize that I need to thank God for?

What did I realize that I need God's help with?

Write a prayer and let God know how you plan to apply these lessons
and truths to your life:

In the Almighty Name of Jesus I pray, Amen

Date:

Who is the author or who is speaking in this verse?

Verse:

Did I learn anything that I can praise God for?

Did God tug at my heart about something I need to confess?

What did I realize that I need to thank God for?

What did I realize that I need God's help with?

Write a prayer and let God know how you plan to apply these lessons and truths to your life:

In the Almighty Name of Jesus I pray, Amen

Date:

Who is the author or who is speaking in this verse?

Verse:

Did I learn anything that I can praise God for?

Did God tug at my heart about something I need to confess?

What did I realize that I need to thank God for?

What did I realize that I need God's help with?

Write a prayer and let God know how you plan to apply these lessons
and truths to your life:

In the Almighty Name of Jesus I pray, Amen

Date:

Who is the author or who is speaking in this verse?

Verse:

Did I learn anything that I can praise God for?

Did God tug at my heart about something I need to confess?

What did I realize that I need to thank God for?

What did I realize that I need God's help with?

Write a prayer and let God know how you plan to apply these lessons and truths to your life:

In the Almighty Name of Jesus I pray, Amen

Date:

Who is the author or who is speaking in this verse?

Verse:

Did I learn anything that I can praise God for?

Did God tug at my heart about something I need to confess?

What did I realize that I need to thank God for?

What did I realize that I need God's help with?

Write a prayer and let God know how you plan to apply these lessons
and truths to your life:

In the Almighty Name of Jesus I pray, Amen

Date:

Who is the author or who is speaking in this verse?

Verse:

Did I learn anything that I can praise God for?

Did God tug at my heart about something I need to confess?

What did I realize that I need to thank God for?

What did I realize that I need God's help with?

Write a prayer and let God know how you plan to apply these lessons
and truths to your life:

In the Almighty Name of Jesus I pray, Amen

Date:

Who is the author or who is speaking in this verse?

Verse:

Did I learn anything that I can praise God for?

Did God tug at my heart about something I need to confess?

What did I realize that I need to thank God for?

What did I realize that I need God's help with?

Write a prayer and let God know how you plan to apply these lessons and truths to your life:

In the Almighty Name of Jesus I pray, Amen

Date:

Who is the author or who is speaking in this verse?

Verse:

Did I learn anything that I can praise God for?

Did God tug at my heart about something I need to confess?

What did I realize that I need to thank God for?

What did I realize that I need God's help with?

Write a prayer and let God know how you plan to apply these lessons and truths to your life:

In the Almighty Name of Jesus I pray, Amen

Date:

Who is the author or who is speaking in this verse?

Verse:

Did I learn anything that I can praise God for?

Did God tug at my heart about something I need to confess?

What did I realize that I need to thank God for?

What did I realize that I need God's help with?

Write a prayer and let God know how you plan to apply these lessons
and truths to your life:

In the Almighty Name of Jesus I pray, Amen

Date:

Who is the author or who is speaking in this verse?

Verse:

Did I learn anything that I can praise God for?

Did God tug at my heart about something I need to confess?

What did I realize that I need to thank God for?

What did I realize that I need God's help with?

Write a prayer and let God know how you plan to apply these lessons
and truths to your life:

In the Almighty Name of Jesus I pray, Amen

Date:

Who is the author or who is speaking in this verse?

Verse:

Did I learn anything that I can praise God for?

Did God tug at my heart about something I need to confess?

What did I realize that I need to thank God for?

What did I realize that I need God's help with?

Write a prayer and let God know how you plan to apply these lessons
and truths to your life:

In the Almighty Name of Jesus I pray, Amen

Date:

Who is the author or who is speaking in this verse?

Verse:

Did I learn anything that I can praise God for?

Did God tug at my heart about something I need to confess?

What did I realize that I need to thank God for?

What did I realize that I need God's help with?

Write a prayer and let God know how you plan to apply these lessons
and truths to your life:

In the Almighty Name of Jesus I pray, Amen

Date:

Who is the author or who is speaking in this verse?

Verse:

Did I learn anything that I can praise God for?

Did God tug at my heart about something I need to confess?

What did I realize that I need to thank God for?

What did I realize that I need God's help with?

Write a prayer and let God know how you plan to apply these lessons
and truths to your life:

In the Almighty Name of Jesus I pray, Amen

Date:

Who is the author or who is speaking in this verse?

Verse:

Did I learn anything that I can praise God for?

Did God tug at my heart about something I need to confess?

What did I realize that I need to thank God for?

What did I realize that I need God's help with?

Write a prayer and let God know how you plan to apply these lessons
and truths to your life:

In the Almighty Name of Jesus I pray, Amen

Date:

Who is the author or who is speaking in this verse?

Verse:

Did I learn anything that I can praise God for?

Did God tug at my heart about something I need to confess?

What did I realize that I need to thank God for?

What did I realize that I need God's help with?

Write a prayer and let God know how you plan to apply these lessons
and truths to your life:

In the Almighty Name of Jesus I pray, Amen

Date:

Who is the author or who is speaking in this verse?

Verse:

Did I learn anything that I can praise God for?

Did God tug at my heart about something I need to confess?

What did I realize that I need to thank God for?

What did I realize that I need God's help with?

Write a prayer and let God know how you plan to apply these lessons
and truths to your life:

In the Almighty Name of Jesus I pray, Amen

Date:

Who is the author or who is speaking in this verse?

Verse:

Did I learn anything that I can praise God for?

Did God tug at my heart about something I need to confess?

What did I realize that I need to thank God for?

What did I realize that I need God's help with?

Write a prayer and let God know how you plan to apply these lessons
and truths to your life:

In the Almighty Name of Jesus I pray, Amen

Date:

Who is the author or who is speaking in this verse?

Verse:

Did I learn anything that I can praise God for?

Did God tug at my heart about something I need to confess?

What did I realize that I need to thank God for?

What did I realize that I need God's help with?

Write a prayer and let God know how you plan to apply these lessons
and truths to your life:

In the Almighty Name of Jesus I pray, Amen

Date:

Who is the author or who is speaking in this verse?

Verse:

Did I learn anything that I can praise God for?

Did God tug at my heart about something I need to confess?

What did I realize that I need to thank God for?

What did I realize that I need God's help with?

Write a prayer and let God know how you plan to apply these lessons
and truths to your life:

In the Almighty Name of Jesus I pray, Amen

Date:

Who is the author or who is speaking in this verse?

Verse:

Did I learn anything that I can praise God for?

Did God tug at my heart about something I need to confess?

What did I realize that I need to thank God for?

What did I realize that I need God's help with?

Write a prayer and let God know how you plan to apply these lessons and truths to your life:

In the Almighty Name of Jesus I pray, Amen

Date:

Who is the author or who is speaking in this verse?

Verse:

Did I learn anything that I can praise God for?

Did God tug at my heart about something I need to confess?

What did I realize that I need to thank God for?

What did I realize that I need God's help with?

Write a prayer and let God know how you plan to apply these lessons
and truths to your life:

In the Almighty Name of Jesus I pray, Amen

Date:

Who is the author or who is speaking in this verse?

Verse:

Did I learn anything that I can praise God for?

Did God tug at my heart about something I need to confess?

What did I realize that I need to thank God for?

What did I realize that I need God's help with?

Write a prayer and let God know how you plan to apply these lessons and truths to your life:

In the Almighty Name of Jesus I pray, Amen

Date:

Who is the author or who is speaking in this verse?

Verse:

Did I learn anything that I can praise God for?

Did God tug at my heart about something I need to confess?

What did I realize that I need to thank God for?

What did I realize that I need God's help with?

Write a prayer and let God know how you plan to apply these lessons
and truths to your life:

In the Almighty Name of Jesus I pray, Amen

Date:

Who is the author or who is speaking in this verse?

Verse:

Did I learn anything that I can praise God for?

Did God tug at my heart about something I need to confess?

What did I realize that I need to thank God for?

What did I realize that I need God's help with?

Write a prayer and let God know how you plan to apply these lessons
and truths to your life:

In the Almighty Name of Jesus I pray, Amen

Date:

Who is the author or who is speaking in this verse?

Verse:

Did I learn anything that I can praise God for?

Did God tug at my heart about something I need to confess?

What did I realize that I need to thank God for?

What did I realize that I need God's help with?

Write a prayer and let God know how you plan to apply these lessons
and truths to your life:

In the Almighty Name of Jesus I pray, Amen

Date:

Who is the author or who is speaking in this verse?

Verse:

Did I learn anything that I can praise God for?

Did God tug at my heart about something I need to confess?

What did I realize that I need to thank God for?

What did I realize that I need God's help with?

Write a prayer and let God know how you plan to apply these lessons
and truths to your life:

In the Almighty Name of Jesus I pray, Amen

Date:

Who is the author or who is speaking in this verse?

Verse:

Did I learn anything that I can praise God for?

Did God tug at my heart about something I need to confess?

What did I realize that I need to thank God for?

What did I realize that I need God's help with?

Write a prayer and let God know how you plan to apply these lessons and truths to your life:

In the Almighty Name of Jesus I pray, Amen

Date:

Who is the author or who is speaking in this verse?

Verse:

Did I learn anything that I can praise God for?

Did God tug at my heart about something I need to confess?

What did I realize that I need to thank God for?

What did I realize that I need God's help with?

Write a prayer and let God know how you plan to apply these lessons
and truths to your life:

In the Almighty Name of Jesus I pray, Amen

Date:

Who is the author or who is speaking in this verse?

Verse:

Did I learn anything that I can praise God for?

Did God tug at my heart about something I need to confess?

What did I realize that I need to thank God for?

What did I realize that I need God's help with?

Write a prayer and let God know how you plan to apply these lessons
and truths to your life:

In the Almighty Name of Jesus I pray, Amen

Date:

Who is the author or who is speaking in this verse?

Verse:

Did I learn anything that I can praise God for?

Did God tug at my heart about something I need to confess?

What did I realize that I need to thank God for?

What did I realize that I need God's help with?

Write a prayer and let God know how you plan to apply these lessons
and truths to your life:

In the Almighty Name of Jesus I pray, Amen

Date:

Who is the author or who is speaking in this verse?

Verse:

Did I learn anything that I can praise God for?

Did God tug at my heart about something I need to confess?

What did I realize that I need to thank God for?

What did I realize that I need God's help with?

Write a prayer and let God know how you plan to apply these lessons and truths to your life:

In the Almighty Name of Jesus I pray, Amen

Date:

Who is the author or who is speaking in this verse?

Verse:

Did I learn anything that I can praise God for?

Did God tug at my heart about something I need to confess?

What did I realize that I need to thank God for?

What did I realize that I need God's help with?

Write a prayer and let God know how you plan to apply these lessons
and truths to your life:

In the Almighty Name of Jesus I pray, Amen

Date:

Who is the author or who is speaking in this verse?

Verse:

Did I learn anything that I can praise God for?

Did God tug at my heart about something I need to confess?

What did I realize that I need to thank God for?

What did I realize that I need God's help with?

Write a prayer and let God know how you plan to apply these lessons
and truths to your life:

In the Almighty Name of Jesus I pray, Amen

Date:

Who is the author or who is speaking in this verse?

Verse:

Did I learn anything that I can praise God for?

Did God tug at my heart about something I need to confess?

What did I realize that I need to thank God for?

What did I realize that I need God's help with?

Write a prayer and let God know how you plan to apply these lessons and truths to your life:

In the Almighty Name of Jesus I pray, Amen

Date:

Who is the author or who is speaking in this verse?

Verse:

Did I learn anything that I can praise God for?

Did God tug at my heart about something I need to confess?

What did I realize that I need to thank God for?

What did I realize that I need God's help with?

Write a prayer and let God know how you plan to apply these lessons
and truths to your life:

In the Almighty Name of Jesus I pray, Amen

Date:

Who is the author or who is speaking in this verse?

Verse:

Did I learn anything that I can praise God for?

Did God tug at my heart about something I need to confess?

What did I realize that I need to thank God for?

What did I realize that I need God's help with?

Write a prayer and let God know how you plan to apply these lessons
and truths to your life:

In the Almighty Name of Jesus I pray, Amen

Date:

Who is the author or who is speaking in this verse?

Verse:

Did I learn anything that I can praise God for?

Did God tug at my heart about something I need to confess?

What did I realize that I need to thank God for?

What did I realize that I need God's help with?

Write a prayer and let God know how you plan to apply these lessons and truths to your life:

In the Almighty Name of Jesus I pray, Amen

Date:

Who is the author or who is speaking in this verse?

Verse:

Did I learn anything that I can praise God for?

Did God tug at my heart about something I need to confess?

What did I realize that I need to thank God for?

What did I realize that I need God's help with?

Write a prayer and let God know how you plan to apply these lessons
and truths to your life:

In the Almighty Name of Jesus I pray, Amen

Date:

Who is the author or who is speaking in this verse?

Verse:

Did I learn anything that I can praise God for?

Did God tug at my heart about something I need to confess?

What did I realize that I need to thank God for?

What did I realize that I need God's help with?

Write a prayer and let God know how you plan to apply these lessons
and truths to your life:

In the Almighty Name of Jesus I pray, Amen

Date:

Who is the author or who is speaking in this verse?

Verse:

Did I learn anything that I can praise God for?

Did God tug at my heart about something I need to confess?

What did I realize that I need to thank God for?

What did I realize that I need God's help with?

Write a prayer and let God know how you plan to apply these lessons and truths to your life:

In the Almighty Name of Jesus I pray, Amen

Date:

Who is the author or who is speaking in this verse?

Verse:

Did I learn anything that I can praise God for?

Did God tug at my heart about something I need to confess?

What did I realize that I need to thank God for?

What did I realize that I need God's help with?

Write a prayer and let God know how you plan to apply these lessons and truths to your life:

In the Almighty Name of Jesus I pray, Amen

Date:

Who is the author or who is speaking in this verse?

Verse:

Did I learn anything that I can praise God for?

Did God tug at my heart about something I need to confess?

What did I realize that I need to thank God for?

What did I realize that I need God's help with?

Write a prayer and let God know how you plan to apply these lessons and truths to your life:

In the Almighty Name of Jesus I pray, Amen

Manufactured by Amazon.ca
Bolton, ON